PROTECTING OUR NATURAL RESOURCES

by Rebecca E. Hirsch

CHILDREN'S LIBRARY

CHERRY LAKE PUBLISHING • ANN ARBOR, MICHIGAN

Published in the United States of America
by Cherry Lake Publishing
Ann Arbor, Michigan
www.cherrylakepublishing.com

Printed in the United States of America
Corporate Graphics Inc
January 2010
CLSP06

Consultants: Sean Gosiewski, Alliance for Sustainability; Gail Saunders-Smith, associate professor of literacy, Beeghly College of Education, Youngstown State University

Editorial direction: Book design and illustration:
Amy Van Zee   Kazuko Collins

Photo credits: Peter Wollinga/Shutterstock Images, cover, 1; iStockphoto, 5; Warwick Lister-Kaye/iStockphoto, 7; Aron Brand/Shutterstock Images, 8; Suzanne Tucker/ Shutterstock Images, 11; Tobias Helbig/iStockphoto, 13; Cheryl Casey/Shutterstock Images, 14; Tatiana Grozetskaya/Shutterstock Images, 17; SasPartout/Shutterstock Images, 19; TebNad/Shutterstock Images, 21; kojik/Shutterstock Images, 23; Martin Strmko/iStockphoto, 24; Shevelev Vladimir/Shutterstock Images, 27

Library of Congress Cataloging-in-Publication Data
Hirsch, Rebecca E.
  Save the planet : protecting our natural resources / by Rebecca Hirsch.
      p. cm. — (Language arts explorer)
  Includes index.
  ISBN 978-1-60279-661-4 (hardback) — ISBN 978-1-60279-670-6 (pbk.)
  1. Conservation of natural resources—Juvenile literature. 2. Conservation of natural resources—Study and teaching (Elementary)—Activity programs. I. Title. II. Series.

S940.H57 2010
333.72--dc22

                                    2009038097

Cherry Lake Publishing would like to acknowledge the work of The Partnership for 21st Century Skills. Please visit www.21centuryskills.org for more information.

TABLE OF CONTENTS

You are being given a mission. The facts
in What You Know will help you accomplish
it. Remember What You Know while you are
reading the story. The story will help you
answer the questions at the end of the book.
Have fun on this adventure!

Your mission is to investigate Earth's natural resources. Natural resources are all over the planet. What resources are being used up? How can overusing resources harm Earth? What can people do to help conserve resources for today and for the future? Follow our field team as they travel around the world to learn about natural resources. Be sure to keep What You Know in mind.

WHAT YOU KNOW

★ Natural resources come from nature. They are things that people use such as soil, air, water, and fuel. Resources can also be living things, like plants and animals.

★ Some resources renew themselves. If we are careful, we can use these resources without running out. Air, wind, sunlight, trees, plants, and animals are renewable resources. For example, when a logger cuts down a tree, a new one can be planted. Some resources are not renewable. There is a limited amount. When these resources are gone, they are gone forever. Metals, coal, and oil are nonrenewable resources.

Air, trees, and water are precious natural resources.

★ Pollution happens when unwanted elements find their way into air, land, or water. These elements may be harmful. They can make people, animals, and plants sick.

We are going on a field trip around the world. We will meet people who are using and protecting natural resources. Join us on this exciting adventure as we report from the field!

We began our field research in the United States. At our first stop, we learned about water conservation. We visited a home in Sacramento, California, where two brothers are helping their family conserve water. They told us that Sacramento is going through a drought, so conserving water is important.

The boys also told us that many people around the world don't have enough water. Some people walk long distances to reach clean water. They fill up jugs with the water and carry them home. The water is used for drinking, cooking, and cleaning. If they need more water, they must walk to get it.

In the United States, pipes carry clean water directly into most homes. Clean water is so near that most people don't think about how much they use. In the United States, an average person uses 40 to 100 gallons (150 to 380 l) of water every day. That is a lot.

Household Water Use

The brothers wondered how much water their family used. With the help of an online water calculator, they totaled their water use. They found out that on most days, each person in their house was using 55 gallons (210 l) of

Many U.S. households use a lot of water each day for showers, washing dishes, and watering lawns.

water. The boys wanted to see if they could use less. They began their water-saving plan.

They started with the toilet. The boys improved their toilet so it used less water. They showed us how. First, they filled two small soda bottles with sand and water. Then they screwed on the lids and placed the bottles inside the toilet tank. They were careful to push the bottles away from the flushing parts. The bottles reduce the amount of water in each flush. They take up room in the tank, so less water is needed to fill it. Now, every time the toilet is used, their family saves a little water.

Next, the boys checked for leaks. A leak can waste a lot of water over time. So they went around the house and looked at faucets. They found an outside faucet that had a slow drip. Their father tightened the faucet and fixed the leak.

They also tested the toilet for leaks. They put a few drops of food coloring into the water in the tank. They told everyone not to flush the toilet. Half an hour later, they checked again. Some of the color was in the toilet bowl. That meant the toilet was leaking. The parents helped the boys fix the leaky toilet.

Over time, leaky faucets can waste a lot of water.

EARTH'S PRECIOUS WATER

Even though Earth is a watery planet, 97 percent of its water is seawater. People cannot drink seawater because it is salty or unclean. Only 3 percent is freshwater. Most freshwater is frozen in glaciers and ice caps. That leaves less than 1 percent of all water for people to drink.

The brothers told us that everyone in the family learned water-saving habits. They take shorter showers. The boys time each other to see who can be the quickest. They turn off the faucet while they brush their teeth. They wait to run the washing machine and dishwasher until both have full loads.

In just one month, they reduced their water usage by more than 10 percent. They are trying to cut it even more. The boys say they want to be careful with water today so there will be enough useable water for tomorrow. ★

Our next stop was a farm in Wisconsin. We were there to learn about soil. We met a farmer who practices soil conservation. He gave us a tractor ride and showed us his farm. We saw fields filled with corn, potatoes, and other crops.

Most people think soil is just dirt. But it is more than that. Soil and plants work together. Good soil allows air, water, and nutrients to reach the roots of plants. This helps them grow. In turn, the plants' roots hold the soil together.

Soil Erosion

Without plants, wind and rain can blow or wash away the soil. This is called soil erosion. The top layer contains the richest soil. When the topsoil erodes, the soil left behind is not as fertile. It may not be good for growing crops.

In many places around the world, soils that were once rich are gone. They have been lost by erosion. The soil that remains is too poor for growing food. People living in these areas often do not have enough food to eat.

Here in the Midwest United States, the soil is rich and fertile. The farmer told us that it is some of the best soil in the world for growing food. This rich soil was built up over

Crops and other plants need fertile soil to grow well.

THE LIVING SOIL

Soil is home to many living things. Earthworms, bacteria, and other tiny creatures live there. Most are too small to even see! But these small living things consume dead plants and animals and turn them into rich soil.

hundreds of years by prairie plants with deep roots. When these plants died, they added nutrients back to the soil. But even this good soil can be lost if it isn't cared for.

This is why the farmer works to protect the soil on his farm. He does this by plowing along the slopes of the hill. He plants rows that follow the curves of the ground. The curves slow the water that runs off the hillside. Running water can erode the soil.

Every year he grows different crops in different parts of the farm. This is called crop rotation. It keeps the soil healthy by changing the balance of nutrients.

After a crop is harvested, he plants a cover crop in its place. Cover crops are plants that are grown to keep the ground from being left bare. Cover crops hold the soil in place. They prevent erosion until it is time to plant the next crop.

If people want to grow their own food, they must take care of the soil. If soil is lost, it takes a long time for new soil to form. It is much better to take care of the soil in the first place. ★

Bare soil is vulnerable to wind and water. This can cause erosion, making the ground bad for growing crops.

Today we stopped at a school in Georgia. The students there are helping to protect another resource: clean air.

We met the principal of the school. She told us about the school's clean air plan. It began when the school received money for old buses to be fitted with new machines to clean up emissions. Emissions are harmful substances that buses release into the air. Some emissions are invisible gases. Others are soot and dust.

Students learned about the problem of air pollution. They learned that cars, trucks, and buses produce emissions. Power plants and factories are also large producers of emissions.

Vehicles such as school buses can contribute to air pollution.

14

Sometimes you can see or smell air pollution. But other times you cannot detect it. Air pollution can make it difficult for some people to breathe. It causes other problems, too. Harmful gases can mix with water vapor in the air. The polluted water falls to Earth as acid rain. It falls into forests and waterways where it harms wildlife and trees.

Some gases in air pollution trap heat from the sun. They are called greenhouse gases. Greenhouse gases are a normal part of Earth's atmosphere. But when too many of these gases fill the air, the atmosphere grows warmer. This is bad for people and wildlife.

The students realized there was a lot of pollution created at the school. They formed a group to fight the problem. One change they made was asking parents to turn off their car engines while waiting to pick up their kids. The students even put up signs outside the school to remind the drivers. This helps control emissions from the cars. Some students began riding their bicycles or taking the bus instead of having their parents drive them. Keeping cars off the roads can help keep the air clean. ★

Our team left the United States and headed into Canada's boreal forest. This massive forest runs from Alaska all the way across Canada. We wanted to learn more about the trees in the forest and how they are used.

We met a team of researchers. They study how trees can be harvested responsibly. They explained that trees give food and shelter to the animals that live in forests. Trees are also made into products that people need. Wood becomes lumber for houses and furniture. Ground-up wood is made into paper.

But trees do more than provide materials for us. They absorb water from the ground and release it back into the air. This makes the air moist and cool for miles around. Trees recycle air by giving off oxygen that people need.

CONSERVING THE RAIN FORESTS

In the tropics, rain forest destruction is a serious problem. Conservationists teach local people how to make their livings by harvesting products from the forests. You can help. Look for chocolate, nuts, and tropical fruits with a *rain forest friendly* label. This means the products were harvested in a responsible way.

Forests provide habitats for animals and clean the air, too.

Trees even help control climate change. Carbon dioxide is a greenhouse gas. Trees remove it from the air and store it in their tissues where it can't contribute to climate change.

When forests are destroyed, trees can no longer help cool the air and store carbon dioxide. Without trees to hold soil down, topsoil can wash away. Flooding and dangerous mudslides can happen. Birds and animals can lose their habitats and may become extinct.

You can do simple things to protect forests. Be careful with paper. Use both sides of a piece of paper before you throw it away. If your town has recycling, you can recycle newspapers and other paper. Buy paper products that are made from recycled paper. All these efforts are easy, and they help protect trees. ★

Our team traveled to visit a research group in Madrid, Spain. The scientists here study solar power. They are experimenting with solar cells that capture the sun's energy.

Using the Sun's Energy

The sun sends huge amounts of energy to Earth. Solar cells capture the sun's energy and turn it into electricity. Solar panels on a rooftop can make electricity for a household. The electricity can be stored in a battery to use on cloudy days and at night. Solar power stations can make energy to power a city. These power stations are usually located in deserts where the sun is powerful.

Today, people use a lot of energy. We use energy to light our cities, power our cars, and heat our homes. Most of this energy doesn't come from the sun. It comes from fossil fuels. Coal, oil, and natural gas are fossil fuels. They are made from the remains of ancient creatures. Fossil fuels form over millions of years.

Fossil fuels create serious problems. Taking these fuels out of the ground can scar the earth and damage animal habitats. It can pollute the land, air, and water.

Solar panels use the sun to create electricity.

When fossil fuels are burned, they give off greenhouse gases that contribute to climate change.

Fossil fuels are also nonrenewable. Once we use them up, they're gone. People are using them up quickly. If we continue to use them at the rate we do now, we may only have enough oil left to last us 25 to 50 years.

Many people think renewable energy is the energy of the future. It does not harm Earth. Renewable energy also comes from sources that never run out. It can come from the sun, wind, waves, and even the heat inside Earth.

Wind energy can be used to make electricity. Giant turbines that sit on top of tall towers capture the power of the wind. The turbines have large blades that spin when the wind blows. This makes electricity.

There are many other sources of renewable energy. Dams can harness the energy flowing in a river. Pumps in the ground can capture heat from Earth. Plants, bacteria, and even rotting garbage are sources of energy.

Switching from fossil fuels to renewable energy will take big changes. But fossil fuels create such problems that we may have no choice. The best sources of energy will be ones that are renewable. Perhaps someday, people all over the world will use renewable energy to make electricity. ★

RECYCLING SAVES ENERGY

Recycling is one way to save energy. Paper, plastics, and cans can often be recycled to make new things. Making aluminum cans from recycled aluminum uses 95 percent less energy than making cans from raw materials. Many towns have recycling programs available. Ask your parents to help you find out if you can recycle in your town!

People can use the wind to create energy.

The final stop of our trip is in New Zealand. We are at the Goat Island Marine Reserve. It is a protected area of the ocean where people are not allowed to fish. We watched a class of children swimming in the water. They were wearing wet suits and diving masks. They were on a field trip to watch the fish.

This part of the ocean was not always protected. A few decades ago, the fish here were seen as an endless resource. Lobsters and fish fed on sea urchins. People caught so many lobsters and fish that almost none were left. Without natural predators, the number of sea urchins grew. Soon, there were too many of them. The sea urchins ate the plants until they were almost gone. With no fish and no plants, the ocean looked like an underwater desert.

Changing the Food Chain

All living things are connected in food chains. When one species is removed, other living things in the chain are affected. What happened at Goat Island has happened all over the world. People have fished so much that many species of fish are at the brink of extinction. This is called overfishing.

Today, we are able to catch large amounts of fish because of advanced technology.

Modern fishing methods are part of the problem. People fish in powerful boats. They travel far out into the ocean and fish in places they never have before. They use sonar to locate fish. With sturdier gear, they scoop up more and more of the ocean's fish.

Today, people are finding it harder and harder to find fish to catch. Many fisheries now catch only 10 percent of the fish they caught 50 years ago. There used to be many cod in the North Atlantic, but they have almost disappeared. Cod may never come back because overfishing has changed the ecosystem. Other North Atlantic fish such as haddock, tuna, flounder, and swordfish are also in danger.

In New Zealand, people took action. In 1975 the government created its first marine reserve near Goat Island. Fishing inside the reserve was banned. Some people doubted whether this would help. But there were big changes. In just ten years, the reserve once again had many fish and lobsters. The area near the reserve had many fish, too. Local people who fished outside the reserve again had fish to catch.

Underwater habitats can recover from overfishing.

THE FISH ON YOUR PLATE

You can help the fish population by avoiding types that are in danger. A few fish that are not overfished are trout, sardines, pollock, and herring. The Monterey Bay Aquarium publishes a list of the fish that are not endangered. You can print a copy at http://www.montereybayaquarium.org/cr/cr_seafoodwatch/download.aspx.

Since then, more reserves have been created in New Zealand and other countries. In 2006, the United States created a large protected marine reserve near the Hawaiian Islands. At 139,797 square miles (225 square km), it is larger than all of the U.S. national parks combined.

All over the world, people are changing how they manage fisheries. In places such as Australia, New Zealand, Iceland, and the United States, people are trying ways to harvest fish responsibly. Reports show that some places that were overfished are now recovering. In other places such as Europe and Africa, overfishing is still a big problem.

People have learned that there is not an endless supply of fish. If people want to continue to eat fresh fish and seafood, everyone needs to harvest sustainably. We must protect our resources for future generations. ★

MISSION ACCOMPLISHED!

Congratulations! You have learned that natural resources such as air and water are necessary for us to survive. We can use resources for energy or to make products such as paper and lumber. Natural resources can be harmed when people use them too quickly. Overusing resources can harm the environment by causing pollution or damaging habitats. You've also learned how people can help save natural resources. People can use less water and energy. They can drive less. They can recycle and buy products made of recycled materials. They can shop for fish and forest products that were harvested sustainably. Congratulations on a great mission!

CONSIDER THIS

Consider other ways you can help conserve Earth's natural resources. By asking yourself more questions about natural resources, you might just start a mission of your own!

★ Are humans dependent on natural resources for survival? Why or why not?

Riding your bicycle can cut down on car emissions and help keep the air clean.

★ How are people harming natural resources?

★ How can using natural resources harm the environment?

★ In what ways can humans use natural resources that do not hurt the environment?

★ Why is sustainability important?

★ What are some other ways you can conserve and protect resources?

GLOSSARY

atmosphere (AT-muhss-fihr) the air that surrounds Earth

conservationist (kon-sur-VAY-shuhn-ist) a person who works to save wild places, plants, and animals

cover crop (KUHV-ur KROP) a crop planted to prevent soil erosion

crop rotation (KROP roh-TAY-shun) a system of raising different crops on the same land in different seasons or different years

ecosystem (EE-koh-siss-tuhm) all of the plants and animals that live together in one place

emission (i-MISH-uhn) a substance that is released into the air, such as when fuel is burned

fertile (FUR-tuhl) capable of making or sustaining life

fossil fuels (FOSS-uhl FYOO-uhlss) fuels including oil and natural gas that are the remains of ancient plants and animals

greenhouse gases (GREEN-houss GASS-siz) gases that trap heat in the atmosphere

habitat (HAB-uh-tat) the specific place where an animal or plant lives

marine reserve (muh-REEN ri-SURV) a part of the ocean protected as habitat for fish and other marine animals

pollution (puh-LOO-shuhn) harmful substances released into the air, soil, or water

soil erosion (SOYL i-ROH-zhuhn) the removal of soil by
wind or water

sustainably (suh-STAY-nuh-blee) done in a way that
preserves natural resources for future generations

LEARN MORE

BOOKS

Petersen, Christine. *Alternative Energy*. New York, NY:
Children's Press, 2004.

Silverman, Buffy. *Recycling: Reducing Waste*. Portsmouth,
NH: Heinemann, 2008.

WEB SITES

University of Illinois Extension
http://urbanext.illinois.edu/woods/

See nature up close in this interactive walk through
the woods!

The U.S. Environmental Protection Agency—Kids' Stuff
http://www.epa.gov/ow/kids.html

More information on acid rain, recycling, and what
you can do to protect Earth's natural resources.

WHAT IS IN YOUR SOIL?

Ask an adult to help you dig a hole in a field or garden. Make the hole one foot (0.3 m) deep. You should see layers in the sides of the hole. Mix a scoop of each layer in a clear jar with a lid. Then fill in the hole you dug. Fill the jar with water almost to the top. Put the lid on and shake the jar. Let the jar sit overnight. The next day, look at the soil. Did it settle in layers? The layers contain different types of particles. Heavy particles, like gravel and sand, settle on the bottom. Lighter particles, like clay, settle on top. Some clay may not settle at all and may make the water cloudy. Very light particles, like bits of leaves and wood, may float.

INVESTIGATE YOUR FAMILY'S WATER USE

You can find out how much water your family uses. Choose a day when everyone in your family is at home. Then investigate. How many times was the toilet flushed? How many showers did people take? How many times was the dishwasher used? How about the washing machine? Once you've collected all the information, enter it on this Web site: http://www.swfwmd.state.fl.us/conservation/thepowerof10/. The calculator will tell you how many gallons your family uses. Are you surprised at the answer?

ABOUT THE AUTHOR

Rebecca E. Hirsch, PhD, writes books about science and the environment for children. A former molecular biologist, she writes from her home in State College, Pennsylvania, where she lives with her husband and three children.

ABOUT THE CONSULTANTS

Sean Gosiewski is currently the program director of the Alliance for Sustainability in Minneapolis, Minnesota. He has worked with volunteers in neighborhoods, schools, congregations, and local governments to make their homes, organizations, and communities more sustainable.

Gail Saunders-Smith is a former classroom teacher and Reading Recovery teacher leader. Currently she teaches literacy courses at Youngstown State University in Ohio. Gail is the author of many books for children and three professional books for teachers.